How to make your own
Recycled Paper

Transform many types of waste paper into your own
beautiful hand-made paper with little expense and a few simple materials.

Malcolm Valentine and Rosalind Dace

British Wildlife Promotions Ltd / Search Press

Introduction

Over 5000 years ago the Egyptians were making a type of paper from the stem pith of papyrus, a tall aquatic plant that grows on the banks of the river Nile. The stems of the reeds were split, woven, then dampened and beaten into flat sheets, which were then polished smooth with stones. Some of these papyrus sheets, or rolls, can still be seen today, their beautiful illustrations barely dimmed by the passage of time, preserved for centuries by the dry climate of Egypt.

The Greeks and Romans continued making and using papyrus, but true paper as we know it was invented by the Chinese and patented by Ts'ai Lun, an Imperial Court official, in AD105. At first he used ropes and old fishing nets to make his paper. These he beat to a pulp with water, before draining and pressing the pulp into sheets which he dried in the sun before use. Later, he started using plant fibres and also silk thread. As well as these materials the Chinese used rags in their papermaking process. Today in the British Museum, some early examples of Chinese paper can be seen. These compare well with modern papers and are even better than the paper manufactured in early Europe.

Until the nineteenth century the methods of making paper remained unchanged, with rags of cotton and linen as the raw material, By the middle of the century with demands for paper increasing and rags in short supply, papermakers started using wood pulp instead.

Since then, paper demands have increased even more and in modern manufacturing processes paper mills not only use wood pulp to produce the end product, they use recycled paper as well. Now there is general concern about the conversion of wild areas into managed pulp-producing conifer plantations. Pulp for papermaking should come only from sustainable forest resources, or from recycled material.

These days almost everywhere you look paper can be seen in some form or another. It is present in a wide variety of shapes, patterns, sizes and textures. Attractive recycled products can also be bought cheaply and easily and it is worthwhile seeking out local suppliers.

Because it is in such abundant supply and is so inexpensive we think nothing of discarding paper once it has been used. Vast amounts of reclaimable waste paper are being thrown away each year. Next time you throw out any used paper, just stop and think. From those early days on the banks of the Nile to modern day times the principles of paper production have remained virtually unchanged. In just half an hour, with little expense and a great deal of fun, you could produce your own sheets of recycled handmade paper. The process is simple and is one that can be enjoyed by the whole family. Children especially get great satisfaction from creating their own coloured and decorated sheets of paper. By recycling even a little of your waste you are creating something of your own and learning about a craft that has been practised for centuries.

Opposite: since the Chinese invented paper in the second century A.D., manufacturing processes have remained virtually unchanged. Today, methods used to produce recycled paper by hand are the same as those used to produce paper in the mills. Here a comparison is made between the pulping, draining, drying and finishing processes to illustrate how the same principles are employed – even though the equipment is different.

Comparing some of the hand-made papermaking processes with those used in the mills.

HAND-MADE		IN THE MILL

Pulping

water

stamp-sized pieces of waste paper

Waste paper can be pulped in a liquidiser.

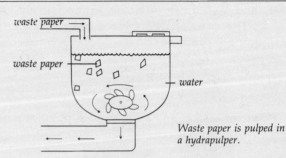

waste paper

waste paper

water

Waste paper is pulped in a hydrapulper.

Draining

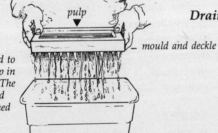

pulp

mould and deckle

The pulp is transferred to a bowl and gathered up in the mould and deckle. The water drains away and the pulp is then couched and pressed.

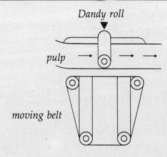

Dandy roll

pulp

moving belt

The pulp is transferred on to a moving mesh belt. A web of fibres is left on the mesh as the water drains away. The web moves on to a series of rollers which press out more water.

Drying

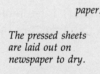

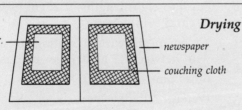

paper

newspaper

couching cloth

The pressed sheets are laid out on newspaper to dry.

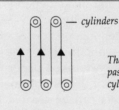

cylinders

The paper dries as it passes over steam-heated cylinders.

Finishing

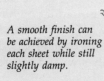

A smooth finish can be achieved by ironing each sheet while still slightly damp.

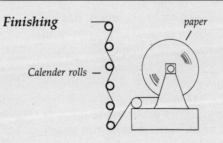

paper

Calender rolls

A smooth surface finish is given to the paper before it reaches 'reel up' at the end of the process.

Materials

Nearly all the materials required for papermaking can be found around the home, apart from the mould and deckle, and a start can be made with relatively little expense. These materials are listed below, with a full description following on.

Waste paper

Newspaper or absorbent paper

Mould and deckle

Liquidiser, or bucket and a long, thick piece of wood

Oblong washing up bowl

Shallow oblong tray

Smooth, re-useable kitchen cloths

2 pressing boards 25 × 20 cm (9¾ × 7¾ in)

Palette knife

Paper

Glossy and heavily illustrated or plastic-coated papers do not react well to the recycling process, but there are not many papers that cannot be used. Waste paper offers many exciting alternatives. The colour and quality of the paper you make depends on the type of paper you choose for pulping.

Office waste is often a good source of pulp because the amount of ink contained on the sheets is frequently minimal. Heavily inked paper will result in a grey recycled sheet, but this is not unattractive.

Lovely white sheets can be created by tearing up photocopier paper, plain typing paper, any clean white paper; even tissues and other absorbent papers can be used. If you add pieces of used blue wrapping paper to the white pulp, the result will be white paper with blue flecks.

Newspapers, although made from a low quality pulp, are readily available. They break up easily when pulped and although they do not make the best paper they are fun to practise with. Carrier bags and paper bags can also be used. If a strong colour is pulped, by adding white paper lighter tones can be created. Once you have mastered the techniques you can go on to try a large variety of alternatives – the choice is endless.

As well as waste paper for pulping, you will require a supply of absorbent or clean newspaper to make your couching mound, (see pages 10 and 11).

Mould and deckle

This simple device is an essential part of the papermaking process and is available from craft shops and suppliers. However, it is relatively easy to make your own and instructions are given below.

The mould is comprised of a rectangular frame across which is stretched a layer of mesh. The deckle is the same size as the mould and is an open frame which rests on top of the mesh-covered mould. The wet pulp is deposited on to the mesh before it is pressed and dried into sheets of paper.

Materials

A 180 cm (5 ft 11 in) length of 2 cm (¾ in) square wood cut into eight lengths: 4 25 cm (9¾ in) lengths and 4 20 cm (7¾ in) lengths

Nylon mesh (curtain netting or similar) is suitable, with between 12 to 20 holes per cm (50 holes per in)

Brass pins or staples

Waterproof adhesive

Nails

To make

Arrange the cut wood to make two frames of the same size and shape. The corners can be mitred if you have the necessary equipment and knowledge; they can be strengthened with brass corner plates or alternatively glued together with waterproof adhesive and secured with nails.

The mesh must be stretched tightly over the top of

A selection of materials.

one of the frames. It is very important that this is as tight as possible. Nylon stretches when wet so dampen the mesh before stretching it. To obtain a tight tension first pin the mesh on the middle of each side alternately with brass pins or staples, pulling as you pin. When all four sides are secured begin working outwards towards each corner, pulling the mesh tight as you fix each pin into the wood. Curtain netting tends to sag after a while, but it can be supported with threads which are stretched across under the mesh.

Finish by trimming away any excess mesh. The mesh-covered fame is the mould and the open frame is the deckle.

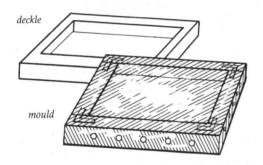

deckle

mould

Other Equipment

A liquidiser is ideal for pulping the waste paper. If you do not possess a liquidiser, the paper can be pulped by hand. For this you will need a bucket and a long, thick piece of wood, or something similar, with which to pound the waste paper into fine particles. If you are using the hand method, soak the paper for two hours before pounding. Remove some of the water and beat the paper to a slushy pulp. This can take quite a long time and the resulting pulp should be fairly smooth. There is no need to soak the paper if you are using a liquidiser.

Once the paper is pulped it is poured into a bowl. In this book an ordinary plastic washing up bowl is used, but any suitably sized oblong bowl will do – or you could even use the kitchen sink.

Using the mould and deckle (see page 4) the pulp is transferred on to a couching cloth. The term couching (pronounced 'cooching') simply refers to the process of transferring the pulp from the mould on to a clean, dry flat surface. Smooth synthetic kitchen cleaning cloths are ideal for this purpose. The couching cloths are used to cover each sheet of pulp as it is made. The sheets are layered between the couching cloths before pressing begins. Coarse cloths with holes are not recommended because they disturb and spoil the smooth finish of the recycled sheet. The couching process is carried out in a shallow oblong plastic tray in this book, but a flat working surface covered with plastic sheeting could be used just as well. The couching mound is simply made from newspaper or absorbent paper.

Pressure has to be applied to the wet sheets in order to expel the water, and two pressing boards are required for this purpose. One is positioned beneath the layered sheets, and one above, like a sandwich. The boards are squeezed together tightly to expel as much water as possible. Make sure you use strong boards that will not bend under pressure.

Many effects can be created by introducing different items and colours into the pulp in the initial stages of papermaking. Natural dyes, poster paints and food colourings can be added to the pulp mix before it is drained, couched and pressed, to produce lovely coloured sheets of recycled paper. A simpler method is just to pulp different coloured papers. Some examples are shown on page 29 (and on the front cover).

Note: when throwing away excess pulp, do not pour it straight down the sink or a blockage could occur. Drain it off first. Alternatively the pulp could be drained, formed into balls and dried. These make excellent 'burning logs' in open fires.

Making the pulp

Tear the paper into long narrow strips. You will need
enough paper to fill the liquidiser approximately six times
over.

Tear the strips into smaller stamp-sized pieces. Place one large handful in the liquidiser. Fill the liquidiser two thirds full and blend the mixture for approximately ten seconds. If you require a smoother pulp, blend the mixture a few seconds more. If you prefer a rougher texture, remove the pulp from the liquidiser at this point.

Pour the pulp into a washing up bowl half full of clean water. Repeat the steps shown on pages 7–9 five times more.

Note The paper can be made more durable by simply adding starch to the water at the pulping stage. Ordinary household starch is ideal, or potato starch (the water left after boiling potatoes) can be used. The more starch used, the stiffer the paper, but normally one or two tablespoonsful are sufficient.

Making the couching mound

It is advisable at this stage to build up a simple couching mound which makes the task of transferring the pulp from the mesh-covered mould to the couching cloths a little easier. Alternatively the pulp can be transferred on to a flat surface. This method is discussed on page 19. You will need a clean, shallow oblong tray. To make the mound, lay a pressing board in the base of the tray. Fold three sheets of paper into small, medium and large pieces. Using the pressing board as the base, layer up the folded sheets with the smallest on the bottom and the largest on top.

Pour water over the paper until it begins to take on the shape of a mound. Moisten it well as it needs to be fairly wet before the mound takes shape. Before starting to make the first sheet, place a damp couching cloth on top of the mound.

Moulding the sheets

It is important to stir up the pulp mixture vigorously and frequently so that the paper fibres do not settle at the bottom of the bowl. If this happens it will be difficult to create proper sheets. Now place the deckle on the top of the mould, which should have its mesh side facing upwards.

Hold the mould and deckle firmly on each of the short sides with the deckle uppermost. Take them down into the pulp mixture at a forty-five degree angle, pulling them towards you as shown.

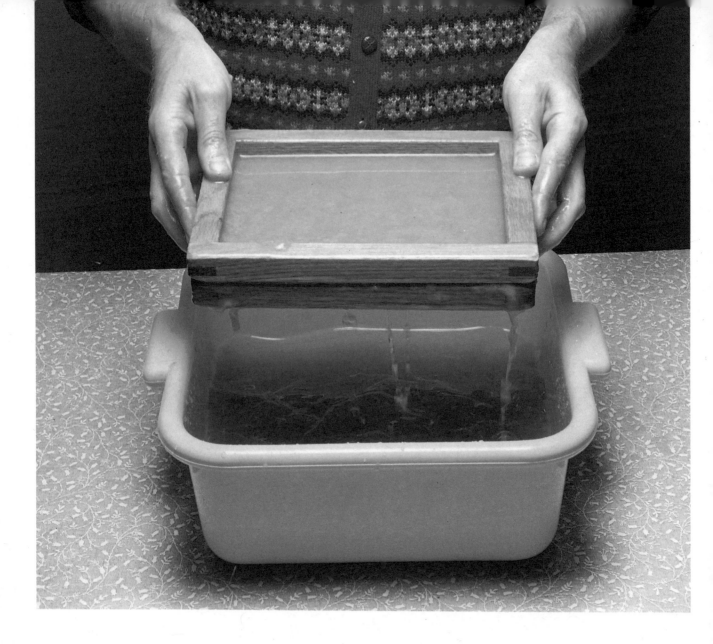

In one continuous movement level off the mould and deckle beneath the surface, then keeping them level, pull them up out of the pulp mixture. The water will drain away through the mesh. While the pulp is still wet, gently shake the mould and deckle forwards, backwards and from side to side. This motion helps the fibres to settle. Do not continue the motion as the pulp becomes less runny; too much movement at this stage will affect the sheet as it forms.

A layer of pulp should cover the mesh. If this is too thin, then add more liquidised pulp to the bowl. Return the pulp covering the mesh to the bowl and repeat the steps until you reach this stage. Wait until all the water has drained away and remove the deckle. You are now ready to couch the first sheet.

Couching the sheets

Transfer the mould to the shallow tray and with the pulp facing the mound, rest the mould on the edge of the cloth, holding the two short sides as shown.

In one continuous movement, roll *the pulp firmly over the mound . . .*

. . . and bring the bottom edge of the mould up, pressing the
top edge into the cloth as you do so.

The pulp should adhere to the mound. If there are still areas of pulp sticking to the mesh, then the whole process of trapping and couching the pulp has to be repeated. The unsuccessful sheet can be simply washed off the mound and the cloth by laying each pulp-covered surface on top of the pulp in the bowl. Replace the used couching cloth with a clean damp one. Re-moisten the mound before commencing.

Alternatively the pulp can be couched on to a flat surface. Place a damp cloth on one of the pressing boards. Press down the pulp on to the cloth, holding the two short sides of the mould and starting with the furthest edge. When the mould is resting flat, gently rub the reverse of the mesh with a dry cloth to remove excess liquid. Lift the mould carefully and rub the mesh where the pulp is still attached.

gently rub the reverse of the mesh with a dry cloth

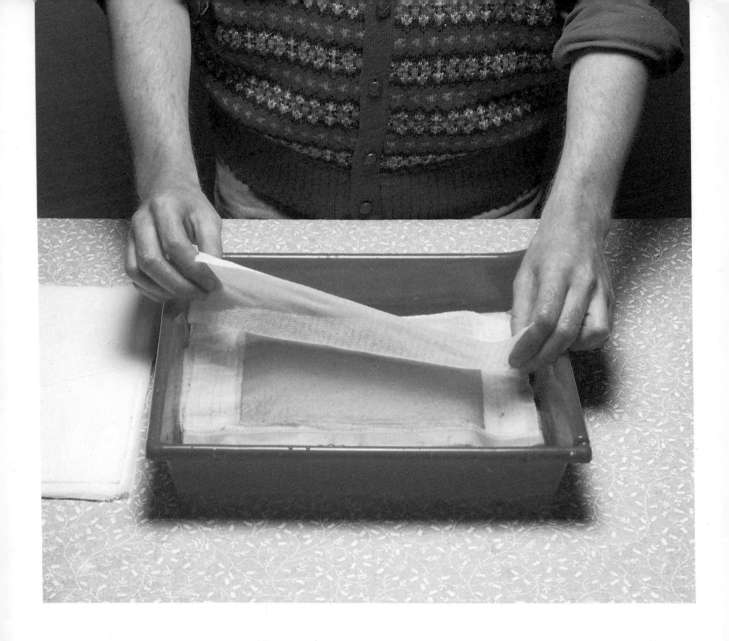

Take another cloth, dampen it and place it on top of the sheet of pulp. Smooth out any wrinkles or these will be forced into the pulp during the pressing process and the crease marks will be visible on the final surface. Repeat each step from page 12 and continue layering the damp cloths and sheets of pulp. Up to twenty sheets can be made at a time. If the pulp becomes thinner as it is removed from the bowl, add more liquidised pulp to the mixture.

Pressing the sheets

When the layering is complete, cover the final sheet with a couching cloth and place the second pressing board on top.

You now have a sandwich with the two pressing boards top and bottom and the layers in between.

Turn the whole stack over. If you have used a couching mound, remove it and replace it with a folded sheet of dry newspaper. Firmly sqeeze the two boards together to expel as much water as possible. The newspaper will absorb most of the excess water as it is forced out of the pulp.

Alternatively, a good way to squeeze out the water is to stand on top of the pile. This is better done outside, but if you are going to use this method indoors, spread plenty of newspaper over the floor first!

Remove the top pressing board and carefully peel off each
cloth.

Do not worry about bending the pulp. By now the fibres will have joined together to form a flexible sheet of paper. The sheets are still wet, however, and they will require a drying period.

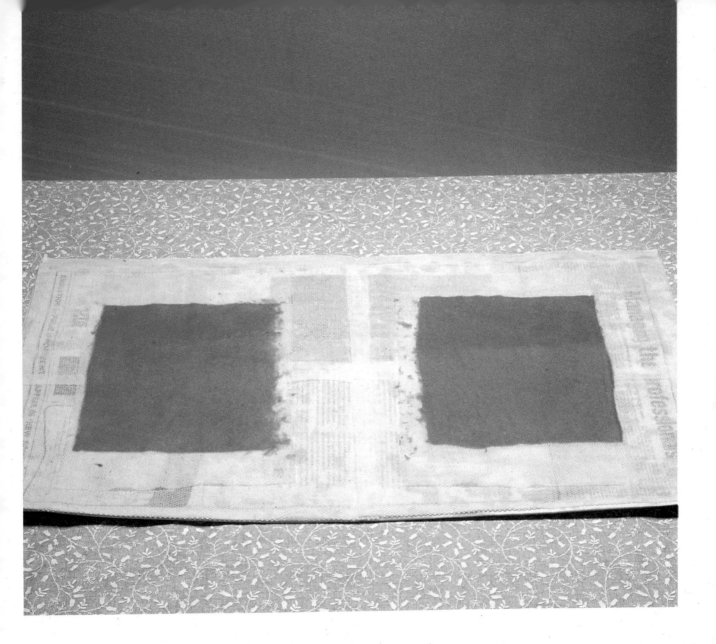

Drying the sheets

Lay out the sheets (still on their couching cloths) on several layers of newspaper. Change the newspapers frequently during the drying period which can take from six hours to a day in normal room temperature. A sunny window ledge will speed up the process.

Finishing off

You may prefer your paper to have a rough surface, in which case just leave the sheets to dry out completely before removing them from the couching cloth. Otherwise, to achieve a smooth, even finish, simply iron each sheet while it is still slightly damp.

Only remove the sheet from the couching cloth when it is completely dry. Gently peel it away from the cloth as shown. It should come away quite easily, but if you experience any difficulty, use a palette knife to ease the edges apart before starting to peel.

Sizing

If you want to use water-based inks or paints on your recycled paper you will have to seal the surface to prevent the colours running. This can be done by applying a weak sizing mixture. For the size mixture you can use gelatine, carragean (moss) which is available from art and craft shops or agar which can be purchased from health food shops. Dissolve half a teaspoon of the size in three quarters of a litre of hot water. Pour this into a shallow tray and briefly immerse each dry sheet in the mixture. Transfer the sized sheet on to a flat plastic-covered area to dry.

28

Adding colour

A beautiful range of coloured papers can be made by simply adding natural dyes or powder paints during the pulping stage, i.e. when you are liquidising or pounding the pulp. An even simpler method is to pulp different coloured papers.

Here, from top to bottom, we have used brown sugar paper; white, blue sugar paper; fawn, pink sugar paper and blue speckled computer printout paper.

Deckle and freely formed edges

Smoother edges are created by using the deckle to trap the pulp as the sheet is being formed (see page 13). These edges will never be completely smooth, because it is impossible to prevent the pulp from flowing between the deckle and mould; also the drying process causes the fibres to contract. These edges are known as 'deckle edges'. You can trim the paper if you prefer, or freely form a sheet by discarding the deckle during the moulding process. Here we show a smoother edged paper (above) and a freely formed sheet (below). The top sheet is made out of discarded Christmas wrapping paper. The bottom sheet is formed from waste cartridge paper; dried flowers are dropped into the pulp before moulding commences – some are mixed into the mixture, the rest are allowed to float on top.

Impressing a leaf

Interesting and attractive effects can be created by impressing leaves, or other items, on to the paper. Here we use a horse chestnut leaf. The sheet is made thicker than usual by adding more liquidised pulp to the washing up bowl in the preliminary stages (see page 9). After all the water has drained away (see page 15) place the leaf on top of the pulp while it is still fairly wet. Couch the sheet as normal (see pages 16–19). Place another couching cloth on top, then place the layers in a heated trouser press. Alternatively, apply heat and pressure by ironing the layers.

When the paper is dry, carefully remove the leaf.

Uses for recycled papers

Once you have decorated and sized your paper you can draw on it, or write special messages to a friend or relative. Unusual greetings cards can be made by gluing sheets of recycled paper to folded card, or beautiful patterns created from several cut up sheets; these can be framed or made into attractive collages. Small labels or tags are an ideal accompaniment to gifts for loved ones. Experiment by making an impression on a dampened sheet with leaves or feathers rolled in ink; or try pressing the damp paper over an object to create a relief impression. Cover the paper with several sheets of newspaper first, then press down hard to create the raised image. Making paper is fun. Use the ideas discussed here to create your own personal gifts and cards.

First published in Great Britain 1990
Search Press Ltd.
Wellwood, North Farm Road,
Tunbridge Wells, Kent TN2 3DR.

in association with

British Wildlife Promotions Ltd.
London House
Pewsey
Wiltshire SN9 5AB

Copyright © Search Press Limited 1990

Photographs: Search Press Studios
Text: Rosalind Dace
Technical Advisor: Malcolm Valentine

The publishers would like to thank David Watson, who was photographed by them during the papermaking process and they would like to thank him for allowing them to photograph samples of his recycled paper, which can be seen on the front cover and on pages 29–31.

The publishers would also like to thank Mr. G. Booth of Paper Publications for providing the reference material for the mill illustrations on page 3 and Mr Anthony Hopkinson, author of *Papermaking at home*, for his help.

ISBN 0 85532 670 0

Typeset by Scribe Design, 123 Watling Street, Gillingham, Kent
Printed by Elkar S. Coop. Autonomia, 71–48012–Bilbao–Spain.